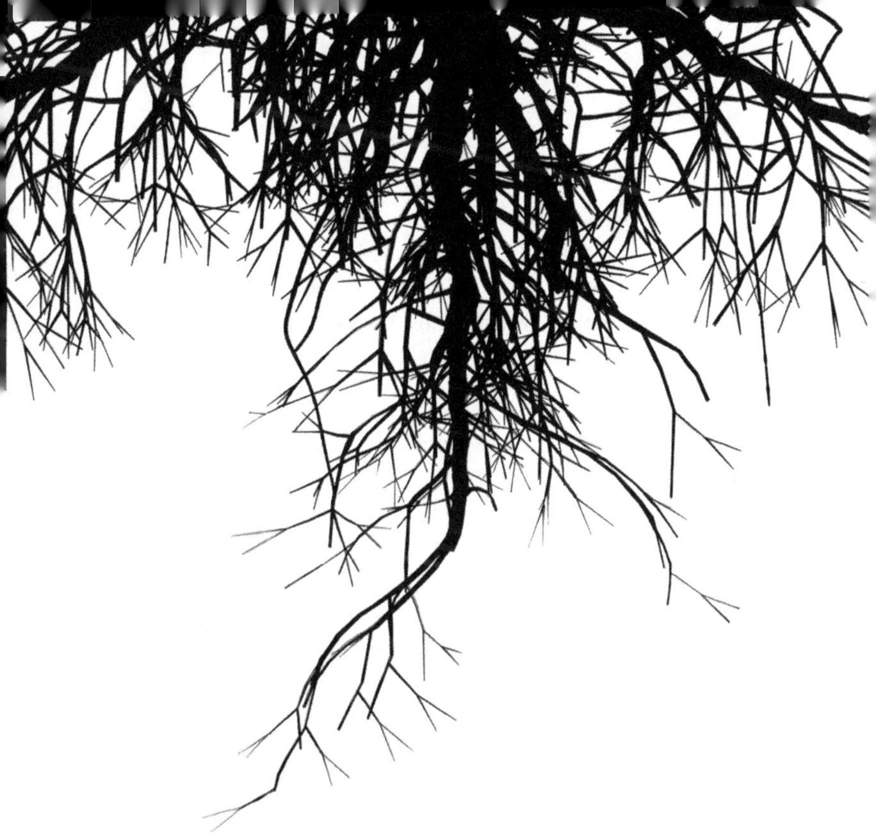

Rooted
IN MY FAITH

The Church of My Childhood

KARLA ELIZABETH BYRD

© 2024 by Karla Elizabeth Byrd. All rights reserved.
Published by Redemption Press, PO Box 427, Enumclaw, WA 98022.
Toll-Free (844) 2REDEEM (273-3336)

Redemption Press is honored to present this title in partnership with the author. The views expressed or implied in this work are those of the author. Redemption Press provides our imprint seal representing design excellence, creative content, and high-quality production.

Noncommercial interests may reproduce portions of this book without the express written permission of the author, provided the text does not exceed five hundred words. When reproducing text from this book, include the following credit line: *"Rooted in My Faith: The Church of My Childhood* by Karla Elizabeth Byrd. Used by permission."

Commercial interests: No part of this publication may be reproduced in any form, stored in a retrieval system, or transmitted in any form by any means—electronic, photocopy, recording, or otherwise—without prior written permission of the publisher/author, except as provided by United States of America copyright law.

All Scripture quotations in this publication are taken from the Holy Bible, New International Version®, NIV®. Copyright © 1973, 1978, 1984, 2011 by Biblica, Inc.™ Used by permission of Zondervan. All rights reserved worldwide. www.zondervan.com The "NIV" and "New International Version" are trademarks registered in the United States Patent and Trademark Office by Biblica, Inc.™

ISBN 13: 978-1-951350-87-1 (paperback)
978-1-951350-88-8 (ePub)
Library of Congress Catalog Card Number: 2023921297

Dedication

Dedicated to my parents, Corbitt and Katherine Puckett. Thank you both for taking me to church and giving me such wonderful memories.

I love you both more than you will ever know.

Contents

1.	Introduction	1
2.	The Power of the Pew	7
3.	Hymns of the Heart	13
4.	The Easter Dress	19
5.	Day of Rest	27
6.	Dinner on the Grounds	33
7.	Importance of a Church Family	39
8.	No Time Limit on God	45
9.	Pass-the-Plate Decision	51
10.	Ride the Altar to Heaven	57
11.	Sunday School Learning	63
12.	Sound of the Bible Pages Turning	69
13.	A Singing Daddy	75

14.	The Prayer Cloth	81
15.	Saying the Blessing	87
16.	Running from Your Calling	93
17.	Church Shoes	99
18.	The Church Nursery	105
19.	Homecomings	111
20.	The Shawl	119
21.	The Back Pew	125
22.	Know Your Faith	131
23.	Baby Dedications	137
24.	Revivals	143
25.	Final Thoughts	149

1

Introduction

Where did time go? It seems like life is going by so fast. As an adult, living in my midlife years, I have to say I am so very thankful for my upbringing. I am thankful my parents saw fit to take me and my siblings to church pretty much every time the door was open. We spent Sunday mornings, Sunday evenings, and Wednesday nights at church. Church was the main focus of our life, as I was a preacher's niece twice over.

Church was our entire family: grandparents, aunts, uncles, and cousins. It was like a family reunion every week. I looked forward to seeing my cousins weekly, and I love that as adults we remain close at heart.

Faith was our way of life. So much of my life involved the church in some way. I have wonderful, happy memories of what I refer to now as the church of my childhood. Those memories comfort my soul in such a special way that it's unexplainable. The feeling of sitting on a pew or praying at an altar automatically brings me a level of peace that is hard to find elsewhere.

My church family celebrated together for all the wonderful occasions of life. Whether someone was getting married, having a baby, or having a milestone birthday, the church family loved, supported, and celebrated all things together. No mat-

Introduction

ter what life threw at me, sitting in those pews helped me get through it. For all the memories I have, today I am thankful.

Why is this book important to me? I refer to the church of my childhood so very often; and I am amazed that when I do, something resonates with someone else. We all have a church memory. Sometimes it's with our own families, as in mine; but sometimes it's with grandparents, aunts, uncles, cousins, the neighbor lady, or simply with friends. My prayer is that this book brings those memories back to life and that you write in the designated areas and share your own experiences.

Why is this important? My son Nick once shared with me that people are only remembered for about two generations. We will also simply fade from memory, taking some memory of history with us.

Writing about those memories helps future generations understand and learn from us. As the church has changed so much in my lifetime, I find it's worth sharing my special memories, which I want my grandchildren, great-grands, and so many more in the future to know.

I pray that when you read my thoughts and stories of the church of my childhood, they trigger heartfelt memories of your own to share. There are empty pages each day for you to fill with your thoughts or memories.

Maybe they are memories of your grandparents or simply things others have shared with you from their years of following our heavenly Father. No matter what the years bring or changes that take place, one thing I know for sure is that Jesus is the same today as he was then.

Introduction

Be blessed, my friends, and may someone in the future be blessed by knowing the same God you know and I know, and may they feel compelled to keep sharing.

~ Mrs. Karla

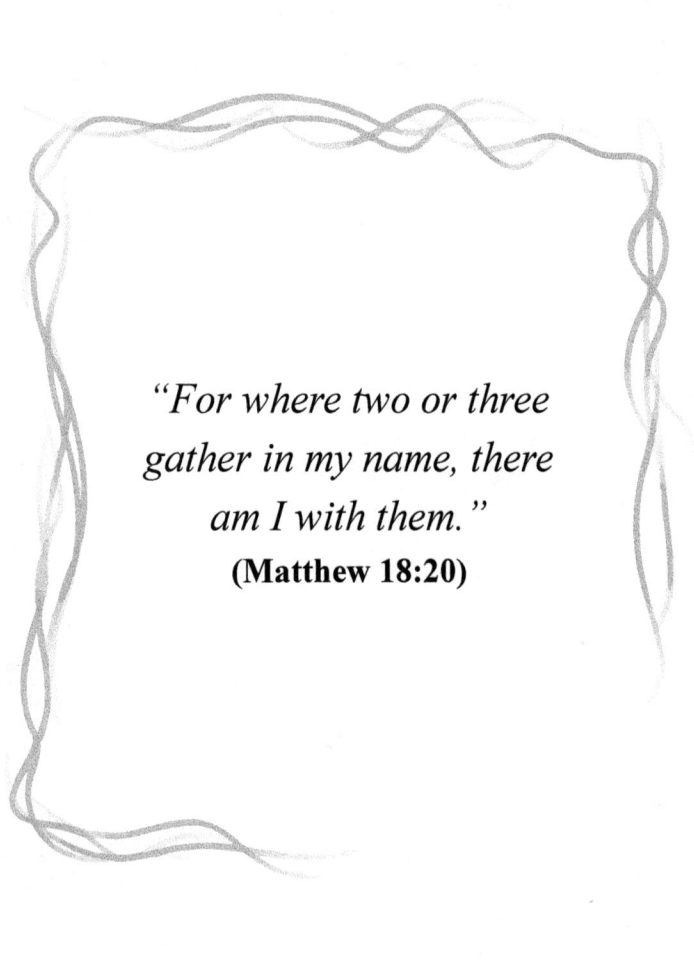

"For where two or three gather in my name, there am I with them."
(Matthew 18:20)

2

The Power of the Pew

No matter what church door we walked into, there they were—the good old-fashioned, never-changing church pews. They were always built solid but not usually upholstered in the most fashionable colors. I have many memories pertaining to the pews.

As a small child, I took many naps on them. When I felt ill on church days, I laid on them, usually covered up by a handmade shawl that marked someone's spot. Their upholstery was usually a berry color, sometimes orange, brown, or a shade of blue; but they all had the same texture when you laid your head on them. From those pews I remember looking up to the ceiling and hearing my Uncle Laney's voice as he preached.

We could fit our whole family on one pew, plus Bibles and bags with plenty of space in between. You could fit all of us cousins on one, as we sat like good kids in front of my Aunt Carol. But we could feel the looks of our parents, their thumbs on our heads or their pats on our shoulders when we were not exactly paying attention.

Everyone had their pew. As in any congregation, everyone sat pretty much in the same place weekly. I know if I looked straight ahead, I would see the familiar beehive hair of Sister Blaylock. Then over to her left, I would see my Granny Puckett. Two pews in front of Granny would be Brother and Sister Matlock. The right side of the church would be filled with the Berryhill family, the Benard family, Brother Ronnie and Sister Brenda Hill, and Granny Hill. And the back row would be my cousin Karen and her family. My parents always sat on the left, second pew from the back.

I knew who was at church and who was missing every week just by looking at the pews. There was just something about a pew that made you know you were in God's house. Something about them comforted my heart and brought peace. Today I am thankful that they hold dear memories from the church of my childhood. Although today most pews have been replaced by chairs, every time I see a pew in an antique store, my heart remembers.

Have you sat in a pew or known a faithful someone who did? What's your memory?

The Power of the Pen

*"Let the message of Christ
dwell among you richly as
you teach and admonish
one another with all wisdom
through psalms, hymns
and songs from the Spirit,
singing to God with gratitude
in your hearts."*

(Colossians 3:16)

3

Hymns of the Heart

"Open up the hymn book to page …" Sister Bea Blaylock would say as she led singing at church each week. Many of those hymns are forever embedded in my head and my heart. There is something about those songs I will never forget.

Maybe it was the repetition, or perhaps it was simply the solid words that went straight to my emotions. Many of them I could relate to and others came straight from Scripture, yet they are all unforgettable. They were easy to sing, easy to remember. I could walk into a church for the first time and know the songs being sung.

I play CDs of hymns in my store, The Byrd's Nest, nestled downtown in our hometown of Gladewater, Texas. The majority of my business is tourists, but many of the customers from all over the country can relate to those hymns. At any moment we will hear people singing along from a corner—possibly two people who don't even know each other—as the hymn takes them back to a memory. It's almost like they just can't help but sing those hymns; those songs are so powerful.

My heart hurts for the ones who aren't introduced to the hymns of my childhood. Those songs are everlasting, from generation to generation. Music has indeed changed. Don't get me wrong, there are some beautiful songs out there; but there's

Hymns of the Heart

something about the songs of old that comforts the soul. They take me back to memories and special people in my life.

I pray you have some of those hymns, which you hold close, and that when you hear them, your heart smiles. I encourage you to turn on the radio, find some old hymns, and remember the words that raised us. Still today, they move me like nothing else. The hymns sung at the church of my childhood will always have a special place in my heart; and I hope when my memory fades, they remain.

Share some of your favorite hymns that hold special memories for your heart. List them and share why they are special.

Hymns of the Heart

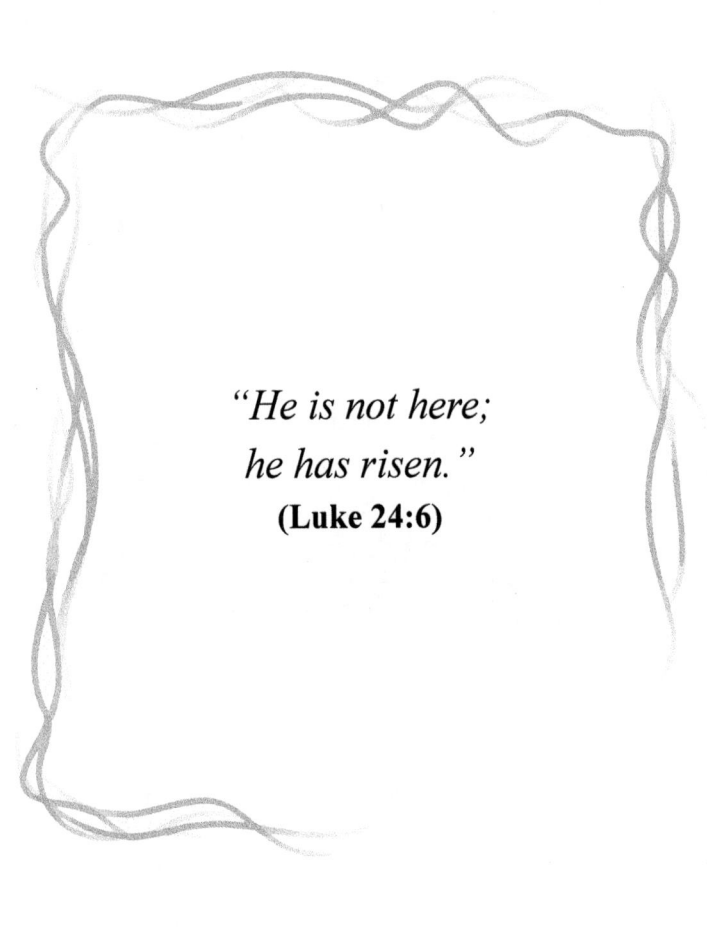

*"He is not here;
he has risen."*
(Luke 24:6)

4

The Easter Dress

Now before I write this chapter, I want to say I hold close the beautiful reason Easter is so important. It's sad to know that Jesus had to die for our sins; but, thankfully, death did not hold him. Our Jesus endured more than what any of us will ever go through in our lifetime.

I am thankful that our Jesus died for me and for you and that he set aside his own wants to do as God directed. As a sinner, it saddens me to know he gave the ultimate for me—little me from Gladewater—a sinner. Now at midlife, I know I am undeserving of his love and sacrifice after all I have done. I am amazed to know he loves me unconditionally anyway, just as he loves you.

Easter Sunday holds special memories. Although we went to church every Sunday, Easter brought everyone to church. Everyone would be there in their Sunday best, and most of the time donned in a new outfit.

It was a privilege to wear a new dress, and it was a special occasion to go shopping for that dress. All of us kids also got pretty shoes that sometimes even had a heel on them, along with those white, ruffled, turned-down socks. Easter hats were big, and of course the Easter basket had to match in some way.

The Easter Dress

I was blessed that some years Mama handmade our dresses, making our Easter outfits extra special. She even sewed us all matching dresses once my daughters were born. Those dresses are truly a wonderful gift of a memory. I still have those dresses.

We were not wealthy people, but we never did without. Both of my parents worked hard, and we always had new Easter dresses, Easter eggs, and a special Easter dinner. Hunting Easter eggs and searching for those valuable prize eggs was such a treat. We always enjoyed dinner on the grounds and, of course, traditional family photos. Those memories are forever in my heart, and I am thankful that I have them to cherish.

On Easter I was always so excited to see the church full and to visit with those I rarely got to see. Now as an adult, however, I understand being in God's house regularly—not just on the holidays—is crucial to my daily life.

Making time for him is vital to my faith. It's kind of like pulling up to the gas station and filling up my tank so I can make it through the week to get where I need to go and do what I need to do. Attending church fills my soul, redirects my heart, and focuses my thinking. It helps me get through frustrating, exhausting days.

A church family is a precious gift our heavenly Father gives us. There is nothing like a family that worships together. That family gets us through some of the hardest times in life when we find ourselves unable to pray and believe.

When I think back on those Easter Sundays, my dresses, and my Jesus, today I am thankful—thankful that I was blessed to have parents who took me to church.

The Easter Dress

Just a note: You can find your heavenly Father at his house every Sunday, not just at Easter and Christmas. Seek him, and you will find him.

Share a favorite Easter memory.

ROOTED IN MY FAITH

The Easter Dress

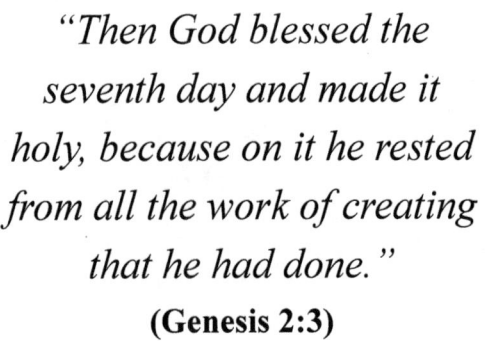

"Then God blessed the seventh day and made it holy, because on it he rested from all the work of creating that he had done."

(Genesis 2:3)

5

Day of Rest

On the seventh day, God rested. On Sundays when I was growing up, pretty much everything was closed. You couldn't shop on Sundays because the mall, shops, and big-named stores were all closed. Sundays were a slow pace and always included going to church, eating dinner together, playing outside, and going back to church for nightly service. My parents took Sundays off, as best I can remember.

My cousin's family always had to take naps between church services. Uncle

Laney was our pastor at First Assembly of God in Gladewater; and we knew if we spent the day at our cousin's house, a nap was a must. There was simply no arguing about it. When I became a mom, I quickly realized how valuable rest was; and now at midlife, I take it seriously.

We have four businesses and a load of responsibility, but we know we need rest to sustain ourselves. Our personal businesses are closed on Sundays, just like Chick-fil-A. (Kinda crazy we crave that chicken on Sundays.) In our businesses, we take Sundays off, although we know it means we are missing customers at our store downtown. We honor God's day of rest, because we now know and realize what a precious gift it is.

Holding that day as God intended is exactly what our bodies need, and our Creator knew it. Sometimes we don't comprehend that what he provided for us is exactly what we need. The older I get, the faster time goes. Days and weeks are fleeting, and it's easy to get overwhelmed. But our heavenly Father provided us all with a day to rejuvenate our bodies, rest our minds, and focus on him. I highly encourage you to make the Lord's Day a true day of rest.

It's a gift to say no to the things that will get in the way of God's blessing of rest. Make your faith a priority, which brings you closer to the Lord, and you will find yourself not missing things like shopping or going to the movies. God's house is always open on Sundays, so consider paying him a visit.

Got a Sunday day of rest memory? Share!

Day of Rest

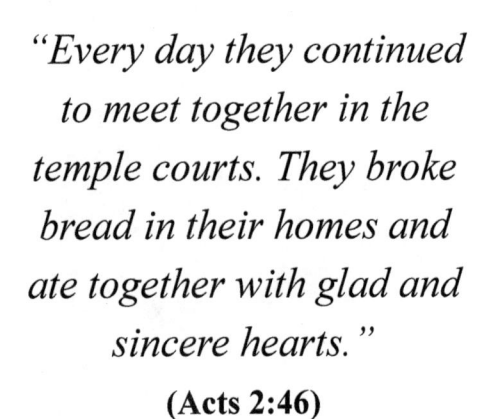

"Every day they continued to meet together in the temple courts. They broke bread in their homes and ate together with glad and sincere hearts."

(Acts 2:46)

6

Dinner on the Grounds

One of my most favorite Sundays was dinner-on-the-grounds Sundays. Why was it called that? It's simply because we ate dinner—you might call it lunch—on the grounds of the church. It meant all the church people brought their favorite dishes, enough to share; and the church families ate together after church. It was a joy and a blessing to be at church till about three in the afternoon, getting more time to visit with our church family.

Now that didn't mean everyone who attended church could cook well. You learned quickly who brought what dishes almost every time. Even as a kid, I knew what was good and what was not so good.

I realized who could cook and who gave it a good effort. I knew who poured their personal, homemade love into their dishes. The homemade dishes were everyone's favorite, so they went quickly, compared to the dishes that were obviously bought at the store on the way to church.

It paid to be the pastor's niece because the pastor's family was allowed to go first in line. Yes, go ahead and laugh, but it was a perk; so thank you, Uncle Laney and Aunt Carol, for serving the Lord. I mean that.

Dinner on the grounds was about so much more than the food. It was quality time spent with church family. It meant more time with my cousins. It was a great Sunday to really visit.

A strong church family is important, and getting to spend time with them is a gift. I look back now to all the dinners on the grounds we were blessed to partake in, and I am thankful. I still to this day do not like pea salad, which seemed to be a favorite for dinner on the grounds, but Aunt Carol's pineapple upside-down cake will always be a favorite that makes me smile!

Ever eat a meal at church?
Remember dinners on the grounds?
Share your memories.

Dinner on the Grounds

"Consequently, you are no longer foreigners and strangers, but fellow citizens with God's people and also members of his household, built on the foundations of the apostles and prophets, with Christ Jesus himself as the chief cornerstone."

(Ephesians 2:19)

7

Importance of a Church Family

Having grown up in the same church pretty much all my life, I am blessed to say I have a strong church family. We worship our heavenly Father together, pray together, cry on each other's shoulders, and love one another no matter our mistakes.

The church family is made up of people in your life who celebrate when you go through life's milestones. They pray you through until you find Jesus, and they call you or drop by if they think you have lost Jesus.

Your church family will shower you when you find Mr. Right, and they will quickly inform Mr. Right what his right place is in your life. They celebrate weddings and shower you with blessings when you are expecting a baby. They encourage you in all steps of your path, and they are always there to help you when you lose your way.

Your heavenly Father uses your church family in such amazing ways, and it's not until we are older that we can see that clearly. Someone is praying for you. Someone knows when you need that hug and encouragement. Someone will meet you at the prayer altar and simply be there to pray right beside you.

Importance of a Church Family

A church family is such a blessing to be a part of, but it's a choice. It's a choice to open your heart and serve alongside good people who simply love the Lord. It's a choice to be a part of a church family and not just sit on a pew. Serving God and serving one another is all about ministry, and it is wonderful to do both.

I hope you smile when you think of your childhood and that someone comes to mind when you think of the church of your childhood. I challenge you to not just be a pew sitter. Get up, shake hands, and join the family of God.

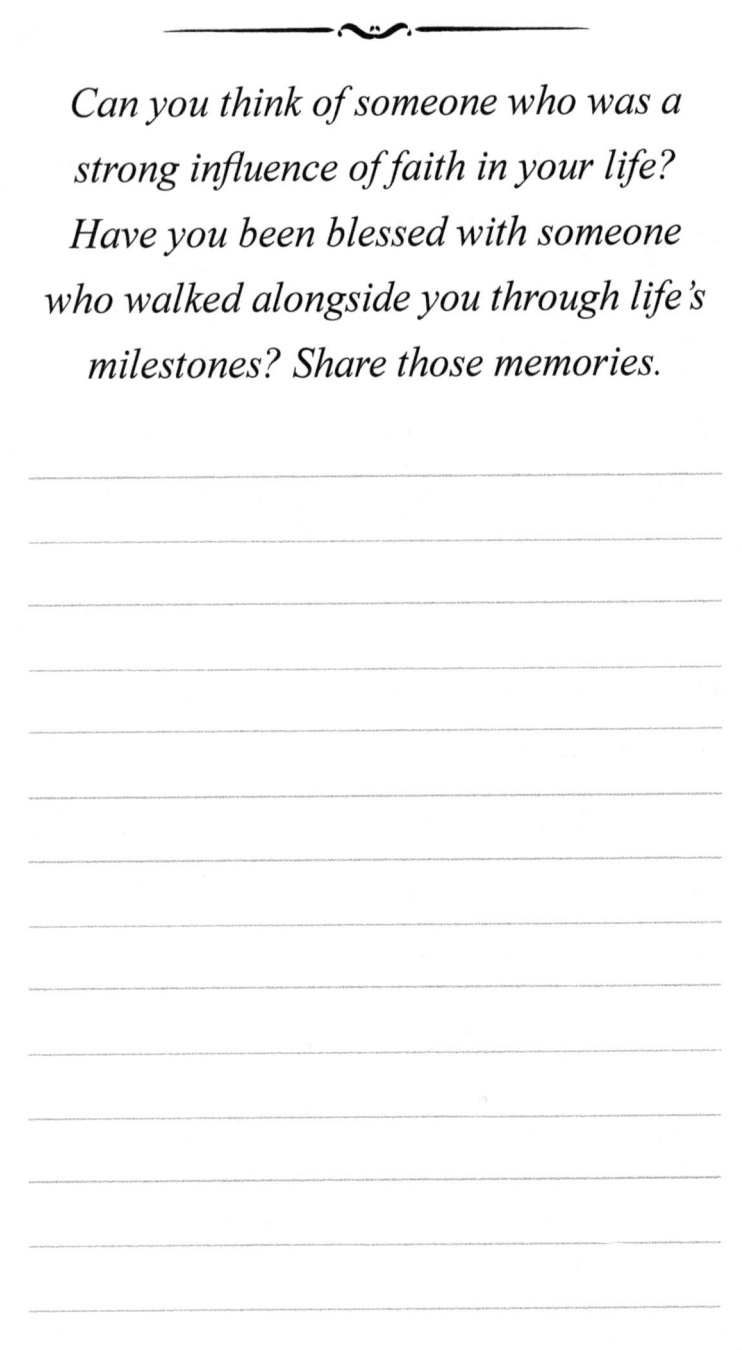

Can you think of someone who was a strong influence of faith in your life? Have you been blessed with someone who walked alongside you through life's milestones? Share those memories.

Importance of a Church Family

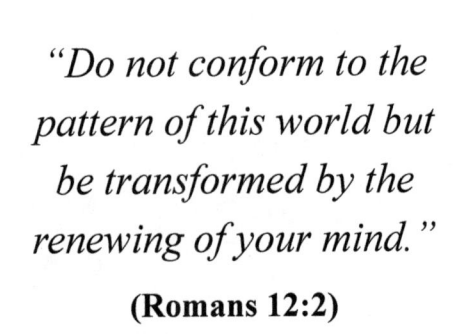

"Do not conform to the pattern of this world but be transformed by the renewing of your mind."

(Romans 12:2)

8

No Time Limit on God

Oh, I clearly remember those services when the Holy Ghost moved, people prayed, and hearts were won for Jesus. I remember there was no real exit time for church services because our heavenly Father was in charge; and in his church, he was free to move in the hearts of those gathered.

Did we get a little hungry? Well, yes, but you knew to eat breakfast or sneak that snack in your pocket. It had to be a snack small enough so that no one would see you

ROOTED IN MY FAITH

eating it because food wasn't allowed in the sanctuary. Did you like to be the first in line for lunch? Well, yes, but Jesus didn't care about what was convenient. Jesus cared for the souls of those gathered in his church. After all, that is why you went to church, right?

Setting a time limit on God shortchanges blessings. I understand reaching the multitudes, but individual souls are most important. I truly don't understand those who set the timer on God, and I struggle with it. I am a farmer's wife, and herding the crowds in and out by having multiple services is just the time we live in, I guess; but I don't understand it. Just build a bigger building.

I once kneeled at a wooden altar and received Jesus. I remember my church family surrounding me, praying with me, lifting my hands, and staying there till my heart was reached. Not everyone receives in a swift manner; but, thankfully, our Jesus is patient. We never stopped praying.

I love this about the church of my childhood. I have searched for that church again in my adult years, and I finally found it at Abundant Life Church in Gladewater. No hurry, no worry. Jesus is here. I encourage you to seek that church that doesn't put a time limit on God. You will be glad you did, and lunch will be ready somewhere when you are done. The main thing is that you spend some time with your Father and get your heart right.

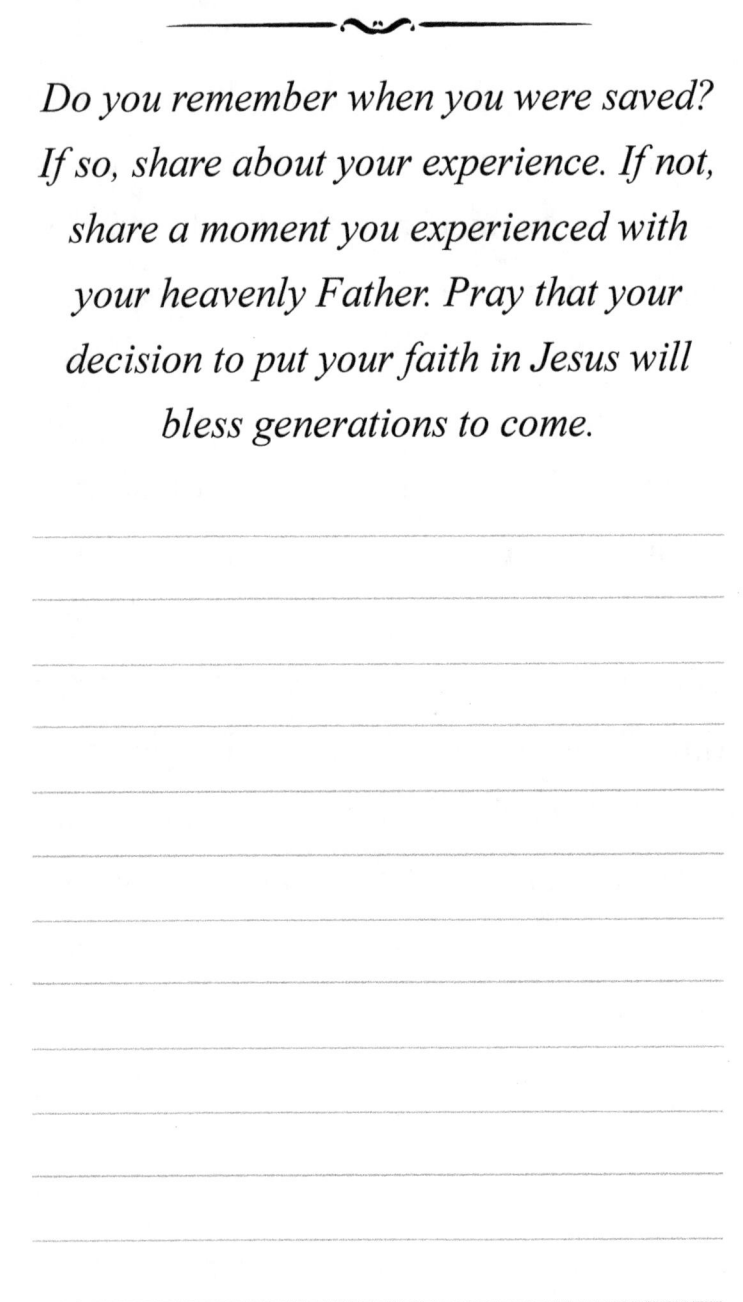

Do you remember when you were saved? If so, share about your experience. If not, share a moment you experienced with your heavenly Father. Pray that your decision to put your faith in Jesus will bless generations to come.

No Time Limit on God

"Remember this: Whoever sows sparingly will also reap sparingly, and whoever sows generously will also reap generously. Each of you should give what you have decided in your heart to give, not reluctantly or under compulsion, for God loves a cheerful giver."

(2 Corinthians 9:6–7)

9

Pass-the-Plate Decision

I never really thought of the importance of giving an offering until I was sitting in a pew in North Carolina watching as a video of church announcements played on the screen. The video included information on how to pay your tithe online, quickly and easily.

Where had the church that I was raised in gone? Didn't these people know it's every kid's joy to help pass the plate? Growing up sitting in church pews and sliding that wooden, red-felt-circle plate like a hockey puck wasn't an option because it wasn't sliding to the next person, guaranteed.

It was exciting to have to get up during church, even if it was simply to go get the plate and keep it passing. Getting out of the pew during church was a treat, and it was also an honor to help with something as important as the offering. We knew our Jesus was smiling because it was an important part of church.

As an adult, I view tithing as a special moment of being faithful to our heavenly Father. The pass-the-plate decision is a choice we make to be faithful to him as he is faithful to us. It's a physical action of obedience, recognizing what the Lord has given us. That simple act of faithfulness is a part of following Jesus Christ.

The church can't run on prayers alone. It has necessities that must be paid, but the act of tithing is so much more. Modern-day times are all about credit cards and online payments, but the next time you tithe—however you give your offering—think of it as being obedient to your heavenly Father. Thank him every week, month, year, or whenever you choose to give your tithe. Thank him for all you have and pray over your offering—that his will be done and his work continues to reach those who need him.

Have you ever had to make a pass-the-plate decision? Giving when you think you can't afford to is a true step in faithfulness. Share a moment when your heavenly Father was faithful to you.

Pass-the-Plate Decision

"Neither height nor depth, nor anything else in all creation, will be able to separate us from the love of God that is in Christ Jesus our Lord."

(Romans 8:39)

10

Ride the Altar to Heaven

The saying "ride the altar to heaven" came from my childhood pastor who happened to be my Uncle Laney at First Assembly of God. I remember he preached the Word and shared key lessons with the congregation that I still remember: life will have trials, no one is perfect and we will fall short daily, our heavenly Father loves us.

He would also encourage those who struggled to simply pray. One of the great things about coming to church is you can leave those worries and struggles at the altar of the Lord. He wants your baggage, your concerns, and your heartaches. Uncle Laney would go on to explain that it didn't matter if you needed prayer every week.

"You can ride that altar to heaven by going to the altar and having a talk with Jesus," he'd say. I heard many times that it doesn't matter how you get there. What matters is that you make it to heaven.

We all know we are sinners. I am a sinner, and you are a sinner. We know when we have made the wrong or bad choice. I personally have made plenty.

The greatest gift Jesus ever gave is forgiveness. He died on the cross for each of us—for you and for me. Yes, you. And he died on the cross for me, my imperfect self. I'm so very thankful today that I can ride that old-fashioned altar to heaven, and I know my Jesus will meet me at the gate.

The next time you're in church and you feel that Holy Spirit nudge, that means you need to pray. There is something in your heart that needs tending to. Don't worry about what others think because they can't get you to heaven; but they can pray for you and with you. So focus your heart on your Jesus and know I am praying for each of you who is reading these words to accept Jesus so you can ride into heaven on a cloud of glory. Praise Jesus!

Do you have a saying that resonates with you from your growing-up years? Share and pray it touches someone else's heart like it has yours.

Ride the Altar to Heaven

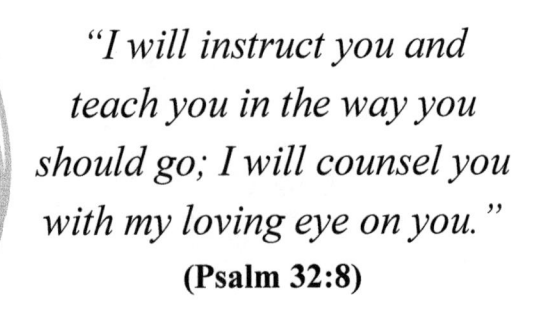

"I will instruct you and teach you in the way you should go; I will counsel you with my loving eye on you."
(Psalm 32:8)

11

Sunday School Learning

A very precious lady named Sister Bea Blaylock was my childhood Sunday school teacher. She was a small-framed woman with big, black, beehive hair; and she loved us all big. Sister Blaylock was a pillar in our church. She led Sunday morning singing, which is now called praise and worship, from a footstool kept behind the podium. As I mentioned, she was a little lady—under five feet tall—but she had a bold relationship with Jesus; and she served him beautifully.

I was sitting in church a few weeks ago and our pastor, Mark Whitehead, started singing a little jingle that I heard every week for years of my life. It was about a little birdie telling you to wake up or you would be late for Sunday school. I am sure there are different versions of it, but it was special to my childhood and forever embedded in my memory.

When Pastor Mark Whitehead started singing it, my heart smiled. I grew up here in Gladewater. Pastor Mark was raised in Louisiana, but obviously somebody sang that jingle to him as well.

My Sunday school experience was a great one. We learned so much of the Bible and had fun studying about the people in the stories. Sunday school helps build a firm foundation of understanding the Bible. It takes effort, and trust me, I know as

Sunday School Learning

a parent everything will happen on Sunday morning to divert you; but take your kids to Sunday school. It's worth investing a little bit of Jesus in them.

Do you have a Sunday school teacher whom you have special memories of or someone who was a strong faith influence in your life? Share from your heart.

Sunday School Learning

"For everything that was written in the past was written to teach us, so that through the endurance taught in the Scriptures and the encouragement they provide we might have hope."

(Romans 15:4)

12

Sound of the Bible Pages Turning

There are familiar sounds that stand out to us as soon as we hear them—sounds that we can identify and know what is happening without seeing anything. The sound of pages turning is forever embedded in my heart. I know that familiar sound is coming the moment praise and worship is over and the preacher takes the podium, giving the congregation the Scripture reference.

Think about it. Long before projectors posted Scripture on the screens or before people had access to the Bible on their phones, everyone brought the Good Book to church. We opened our Bibles, thumbed through the pages, and followed along as the preacher read the words. I am thankful for these moments that taught me to open the Good Book.

Now, many years later, when I hand out a devotional or a Bible, I look people straight in the eye and tell them to open the Book. I learned to seek answers by opening the Book. I learned to open my heart to the Word of God and receive guidance by opening the Book.

The rustling sound of pages turning in those moments as the preacher begins his sermon is simply a sound that is special to me. Anyone can look up at words on a big screen, but I am thankful that as a child I learned to open my Bible. It taught me to find Scriptures and the words I seek.

The Bible is applicable to all avenues of your life's journey, and that is the beautiful way the Lord designed it. At a young age, that familiar sound of pages turning taught me to open the Book and apply it to my life as I follow my Jesus Christ.

Next time you attend church, take your Bible. Teach your children to open their Bibles and seek direction for their lives, and they will find answers to their questions. This is one lesson you can teach them that will last a lifetime and, prayerfully, transfer to future generations.

Are there sounds you identify instantly that take you back to memories you hold dear? Do you know where to find the answers you seek in life? I pray you have learned to open the Book. Share your memories.

Sound of the Bible Pages Turning

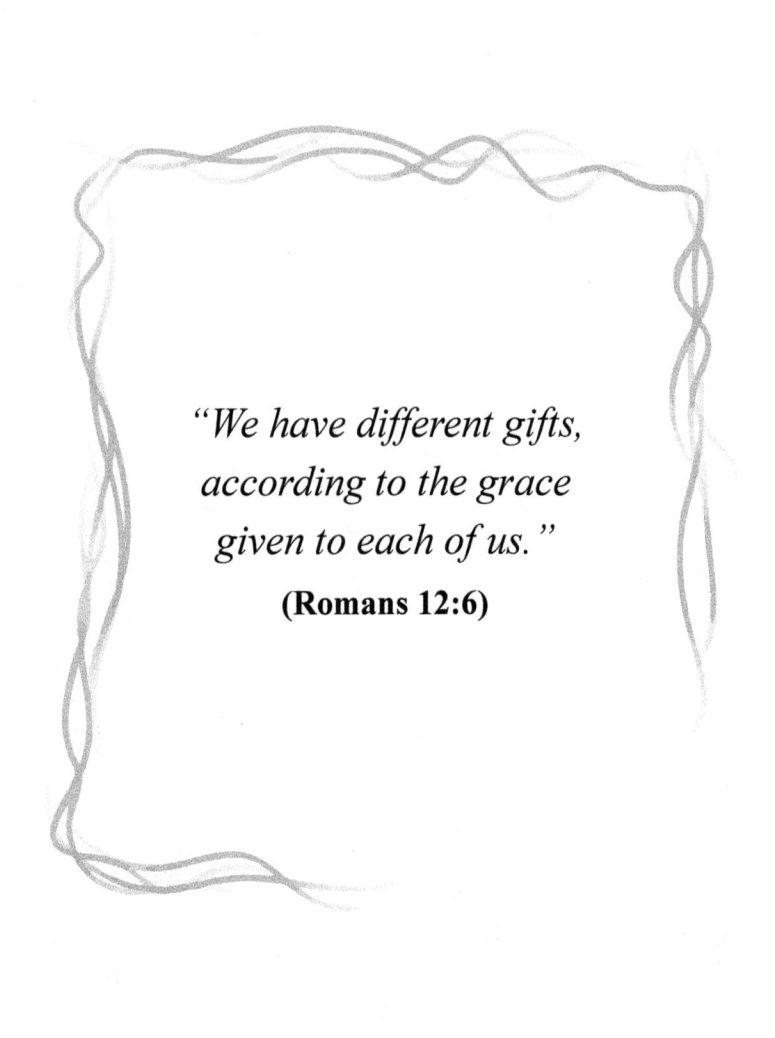

"We have different gifts, according to the grace given to each of us."

(Romans 12:6)

13

A Singing Daddy

I grew up with a singing daddy. My dad could sing anything he wanted. His low, strong alto voice was bold but smooth. I can't recall very many days Daddy wasn't singing in church. He led worship, sang specials, and lent his voice to background vocals to countless others who maybe weren't as confident. He had a gift, no doubt about it. He sang with confidence and ministered to the hearts of many through music.

Daddy could sing; and when he would bust out with fast songs, like "Goodbye World, Goodbye," he would take the congregation to another level of praise. His vocals could make even the people in the back pew feel the Holy Spirit. He could bring a congregation to their feet with hands in the air, all worshipping their Jesus.

I was privileged to have parents who taught me the confidence to sing. They encouraged me; and at a young age, I had a song in my heart and a microphone in my hand.

Words of songs can move your heart, opening it up so the Holy Spirit can move within you. Lyrics can take you to a higher level of emotion and can strengthen your faith. Songs can prepare you for the battles of the day and set your step to real joy.

A Singing Daddy

They can make you worship your Jesus in such a way just speaking words can't.

One of my favorite things to sing is the hymns from my childhood. Those hymns were so moving, and they would make even the toughest sinner know Jesus.

I encourage you to turn your radio to Christian music and make Jesus more a part of your day. Turn on the local Christian radio station at work. Even if you're not singing it, hearing it will bless you. The local station here does a challenge. They challenge you to simply turn them on over a period of time and see if it makes a difference in your life. Why not try it?

Is there a song that moves you to praise? Do you have a memory of someone who used their gift of music to reach your heart? Share your memory.

A Singing Daddy

"Is anyone among you sick? Let them call the elders of the church to pray over them and anoint them with oil in the name of the Lord."
(James 5:14)

14

The Prayer Cloth

It wasn't until about five years ago that this memory came to light in the real beauty of its meaning. When I was growing up in church, I would see my Uncle Laney and the others in the church pray over a simple piece of fabric for someone who was unable to attend church that service.

Maybe they were sick or had other health issues, which made it physically impossible to be there; so the church people would anoint the cloth with oil, hold it in their hands, and pray. That cloth would then be delivered to the person who was ill as a physical reminder that someone was praying for them. They would hold it in their hand, tuck it under their pillow, or simply keep it nearby.

Physical reminders are such sweet blessings. As an adult, I see the true meaning of a mailed card versus a quickly sent email or text message. A card is a reminder that someone is thinking of you. It's touching that someone went through the trouble to buy it, sign it, and mail it. It serves as a physical reminder that someone is thinking of you, and you can open it to receive that blessing as many times as you need.

The prayer cloth has the same touching reminder, except it's a reminder that someone is taking you in prayer to their heavenly Father. How wonderful is that!

The Prayer Cloth

I asked one of my precious store vendors, Terran Turner from The Byrd's Nest, to make a little praying-for-you pillow for her booth. She makes hand-stitched quilt pillows, which are one of my favorite things at the store. It touches me every time I see someone purchase one of those special little pillows because I know it will reach someone's heart.

Sometimes the only thing someone really needs to help them with what they are going through is your prayers. Think about sending a card to someone who may need it today, and simply remind them you are praying for them.

Have you ever received a special gift that reached deep into your heart? Perhaps you were given a card or a gift that made an impact. Share that memory.

The Prayer Cloth

"After he said this, he took some bread and gave thanks to God in front of them all. Then he broke it and began to eat."

(Acts 27:35)

15

Saying the Blessing

One of the first prayers I learned in my life was saying the blessing over the food. I can't think of one meal we ever ate that wasn't prayed over. I think it was one of the first habits I developed. Goodness we couldn't eat until the blessing was said; and at times, that was a struggle. It didn't matter where we were, who we were with, or if we were starving, because we weren't eating until the amen.

Why was this prayer so important? Simply because it instilled thankfulness in our hearts in a way that little ones understand. It was about knowing that our heavenly Father provided for our family, and it reminded us to be thankful. I raised my kids with the same mindset of thankfulness. We said the blessing no matter who else was at the supper table. As an adult, I still can't eat without the blessing being said.

Breakfast, lunch, dinner, and snacks are all provisions. Our heavenly Father knew the bodies he created would need nourishment. He knew what we needed before we were even created because we were designed by him. It's easy to be in a hurry or struggling with the kids or just running short on time; but remember, all that you have is a provision, so teach your family that and be thankful.

Do you remember the first prayers you learned? What prayers hold a special meaning to you?

ROOTED IN MY FAITH

Saying the Blessing

"For we are God's handiwork, created in Christ Jesus to do good works, which God prepared in advance for us to do."

(Ephesians 2:10)

16

Running from Your Calling

All my life, I was taught that each one of us was created for a purpose. I learned that we all have a calling upon our lives, and that as we journey through life, that calling would come forth, and the Lord would use each of us to do his work in the world.

I remember watching a young man in our church who was just a few years older than I was give his first sermon. In fact, in my little red, zipper Bible, I wrote his name and the date with a notation that it was his first sermon. I have used something he shared in his sermon that day so many times in my life, and I think of him every time I say it.

He referred to Scripture and mentioned that the Bible clearly says to obey the laws of the land. He used the example that when we go above the posted speed limit, we're sinning. I shared that sermon note many times with my lead-footed children when they started learning to drive.

So many times in life, we struggle to figure out our calling. We may wonder why we are here and why we were created. I assure you that you have a calling. Sometimes it's hard to see. Sometimes it's not exactly what we think we should be doing. Sometimes we're called to small things while others are called to big things.

Nonetheless, we all have a part in God's creation, and we all have a calling upon our lives.

Your calling started long before you were born. Some run from it or fail to recognize it, but the beautiful thing is that our heavenly Father never gives up on you. He pursues you until you accept him and his purpose for your life. So next time you're in a season of feeling like you have no purpose, I encourage you to pour into your heart. Take that time to pour into your soul, study the Word, and simply ask him to show you clearly what he wants of your life. The hard part is being quiet and listening.

Do you know God's calling on your life? Or is there a calling that you have run from and never accepted? If so, know he is waiting for you to simply say yes.

Running from Your Calling

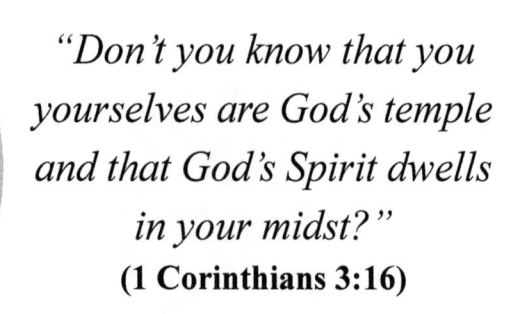

"Don't you know that you yourselves are God's temple and that God's Spirit dwells in your midst?"
(1 Corinthians 3:16)

17

Church Shoes

I remember the pure joy of getting to go pick out that special pair of church shoes. Y'all know about church shoes. They were the dressy shoes you weren't allowed to wear to school, outside, or anywhere else but the Lord's house. They were special and matched just about every outfit you wore to church. They were the best of the best you had, and they were usually kept in a special place, such as a closet or in their original box.

If they got scuffed or dirty, you cleaned them. It was an honor to have them, much less wear them. In fact, I was glad to go to church because I got to wear my church shoes. I know the Lord didn't care about those shoes because he was simply glad we were in his house, but I loved them and loved wearing them.

Today I am saddened with the generation we live in. We wore our Sunday best to visit God's house, but casual wear has taken over. My heart hurts at all the little girls who won't know the excitement of church shoes, much less the ones with the heel on them. Again, I know the Lord doesn't really care what we wear because he's just glad we are there.

But I challenge you to put on your best for the Lord. He will honor your heart and effort. Going to his house is different from going to the local grocery store or the mall. I encourage you to not only make going to church a priority but also to make it special for your family. Go against today's norms and choose a pair of church-only shoes. You will seek every reason to go to church.

Give your God your best. Make him and his house a priority. Just as with the Christian music challenge, I challenge you to make a point of doing just a bit extra with your appearance for Jesus. Give your children an example to follow.

Do you have a special memory of a church outfit or shoes? Share.

Church Shoes

"Jesus said, 'Let the little children come to me, and do not hinder them, for the kingdom of heaven belongs to such as these.'"

(Matthew 19:14)

18

The Church Nursery

As church kids, we absolutely couldn't wait till we hit that age when we could help with the church nursery. That milestone birthday meant we were now old enough to help take care of cute little babies and play with toddlers and toys. We were honored to miss big church and help with the little children. We were so excited to get to be in that nursery for so many reasons, but the crackers and snacks were a bonus.

Now as an adult, I see that for many of us, it was our first experience working for the Lord. We were serving in ministry, although we didn't really realize its meaning at the time. Serving in your church is vitally important. There is no job that is too small or too big. As Pastor Mark Whitehead says, "It's your church, our church together."

Serving in your church is a ministry—the hands extended of our heavenly Father. Some Christians have talents beyond talents, while others have that one special thing they know how to do, and they do it well. Not all of us were called to preach to the multitudes or sing special music with the choir, but we are all called to serve our Lord Jesus.

It kind of goes back to that purpose we were each specifically created to do. You and I were designed with purpose in mind, but you know what? We must train our hearts and eyes to see the open doors before us, and we have to learn to say yes.

Saying yes to something out of your comfort zone can be hard; but know your Jesus is right beside you, guiding you in the direction you need to go. Can I go back to the fact that saying yes isn't always easy?

I often tell my customers that my Jesus had a sense of humor by giving me an open door for a store downtown. I clearly see he had a plan all along. And his plan wasn't about me but, instead, about the people walking into The Byrd's Nest who need a reminder that he is their Jesus and they have a purpose.

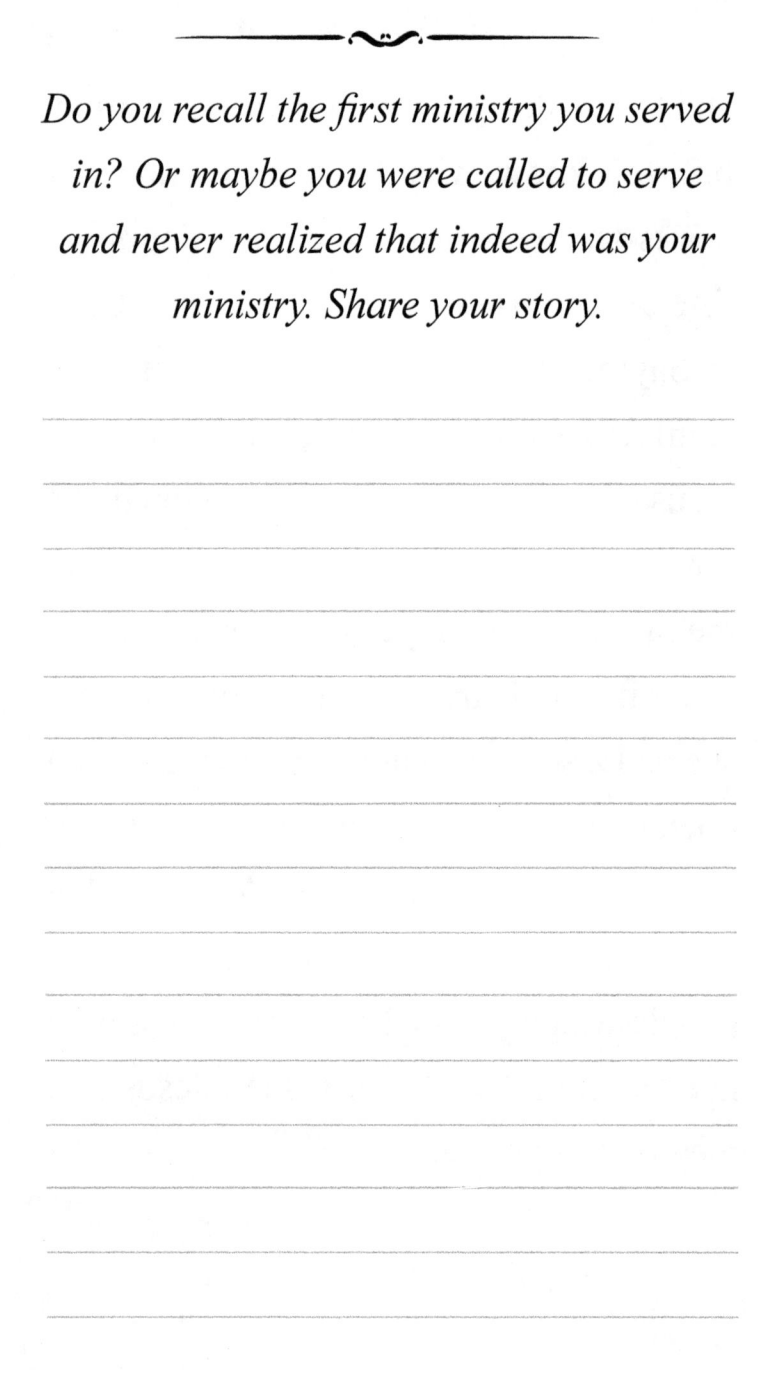

Do you recall the first ministry you served in? Or maybe you were called to serve and never realized that indeed was your ministry. Share your story.

The Church Nursery

"Israel said to Joseph, 'I never expected to see your face again, and now God has allowed me to see your children too.'"

(Genesis 48:11)

19

Homecomings

I was raised with Bapticostal grandparents. My granddad, Papa Puckett, attended a small, white, wooden Baptist church. My grandmother, Granny Puckett, was raised in the Assembly of God, a Pentecostal church. They would attend Woodland Baptist every Sunday morning and Oak Grove Assembly on Sunday nights.

Out of their marriage, my Uncle Don was an Assembly of God preacher; my aunt married my Uncle Laney, an Assembly of God preacher; and Daddy attended an Assembly of God church and ministered in music like a true Pentecostal singer.

Every so many years, Woodland Baptist would hold Homecoming Sunday, a gathering for everyone who attended or who had a family history with the church. It was essentially a meet and greet, complete with dinner on the grounds. Singers would sing specials, including myself; and there would be preaching.

This Sunday was special because my Papa Puckett attended there all his life, and it was always special to visit his church. He was always so proud to have all of us with him. Oh, the food. Let's just say homemade, from scratch. Goodness! The back area of the church was small, but everyone squeezed together at the red plaid tablecloths and ate together.

Memories like these are precious gifts. It's been a long time since I knew of an old-fashioned church hosting a Homecoming Sunday for all who had once gathered there, but to imagine the lives touched within the walls of that old church is something that warms my heart.

It doesn't matter where you attend church, but what matters is that you take ownership of it being your church—the church that leaves everlasting Jesus in the hearts of so many. I am thankful for my growing-up church memories, which are sweet blessings to me now.

I encourage you to find a church family. No matter where you attend, connect. Connecting and becoming a part of a church is a choice and will bless you during all stages of life. It's vital to surround yourself with those who share your same faith.

ROOTED IN MY FAITH

If you're a new Christian and just starting your walk with Christ, let me assure you, being a part of a church family will help you grow your faith. Having brothers and sisters in the family of God will help you in so many ways.

Again, it's a choice to be a part, so get off your duff and shake hands. Meet and greet and connect. Reach out to those who attend with you and make a connection. You will be blessed to be involved with your church.

I believe it takes all of us to use what God created us for to further reach the ones who need Jesus. The mission field is outside the walls of the church, so fill yourself up with the love of God so you can pour out upon others you meet.

Homecoming at Papa's church is such a sweet memory. So many years of ministry were brought to life through the walls of that little church. I pray one day you look back at your home church and feel the same about those walls.

And I encourage you again with this last word: connect.

Do you have a church you visited or attended during the course of your life that impacted you and touched you? Share.

_____

_____

_____

_____

_____

_____

_____

ROOTED IN MY FAITH

Homecomings

"Likewise, teach the older women to be reverent in the way they live, not to be slanderers or addicted to much wine, but to teach what is good. Then they urge the younger women to love their husbands and children."

(Titus 2: 3–4)

20

The Shawl

Handmade, delicate, neatly folded shawls of many colors served as pew markers. These treasures were left weekly in various places in the sanctuary. A shawl let you know that was the place of Sister So-and-So, so don't even think of sitting there. And you could guarantee the owner of the shawl would offer it to any little one in a dress to cover her legs if she decided to take a pew nap.

Those precious shawls marked the places of some of the most powerful praying women I have ever known. Sister Bea Blaylock, Sister Opal Thomas, Sister Humpheries, and so many more sat in those places; and they were strong anchors for our church. They would pray for us, teach us, and love us no matter what.

As an adult, I have grown to appreciate those ladies more than I ever did as a child. Those ladies showered me with kind cards and gifts as I prepared for marriage and babies. They cooked unbelievable food for dinner on the grounds on Sundays. They were strong pillars of faith and beautiful examples of godly women. I never heard anything come forth from them that wasn't good.

Today when I sit in church and look to my right, I see there are strong women of God sitting in those chairs worshipping their heavenly Father. It takes me back to

The Shawl

the church of my childhood, as I reflect on those shawls sitting on the pews. I am so thankful for all the women in my life who have served as examples, and I am honored to follow.

I encourage you to visit with the ladies in your life who have a strong Christian faith. Sit with them and visit, ask questions, and simply ask them about their Jesus. Take time to learn from the strongest of the strong when it comes to ministry, faith, and Jesus Christ.

Does a strong woman of faith come to your mind? Is there someone in your life who has always been a faithful prayer warrior or someone you could look to? Share.

The Shawl

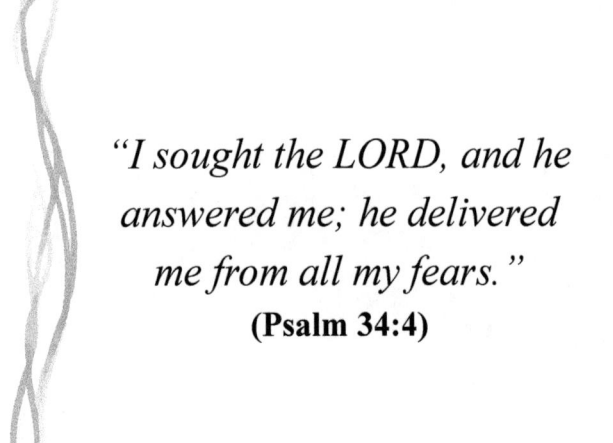

"I sought the LORD, and he answered me; he delivered me from all my fears."
(Psalm 34:4)

21

The Back Pew

In every church there is a back-row pew that seems to be the most popular place in the sanctuary. When you walked through the church doors, you could immediately find a place nestled in the back where you could see the whole view of the sanctuary.

In my mind, the back pew is reserved for a very special person, my Aunt Carol. I can't think of a Sunday growing up that she did not occupy her place on that back pew. She had the best view. She knew who was doing what, even when some of us weren't doing it right. You could feel her look through the back of your head, and you knew she was watching you. She counted attendance for the board in the foyer from that pew. She gave signals to Uncle Laney from that pew if he was going a little long with his preaching. That back row was a powerful seat for a powerful woman of God. For Aunt Carol, I am thankful.

Now as an adult, I am more a front-row kind of Christian. I like to be where I can see, hear, and focus. I have heard a few times that closer to the front means closer to God, but I know that back row is just as powerful as the front.

It doesn't matter where you sit in church. Your heart is what matters. You get out of church what you put into it. In other words, if you come expecting a blessing, you will receive a blessing. When you open yourself to worship the heavenly Father in the right spirit, you invite him to enter and do his work in your life—work that only he can do. You simply must ask him.

The next time you walk into your church, I suggest taking a moment to invite him into your heart. Simply receive what he has for you. It really doesn't matter where you sit; it's just the fact that you came. And trust me, you will be blessed because you did.

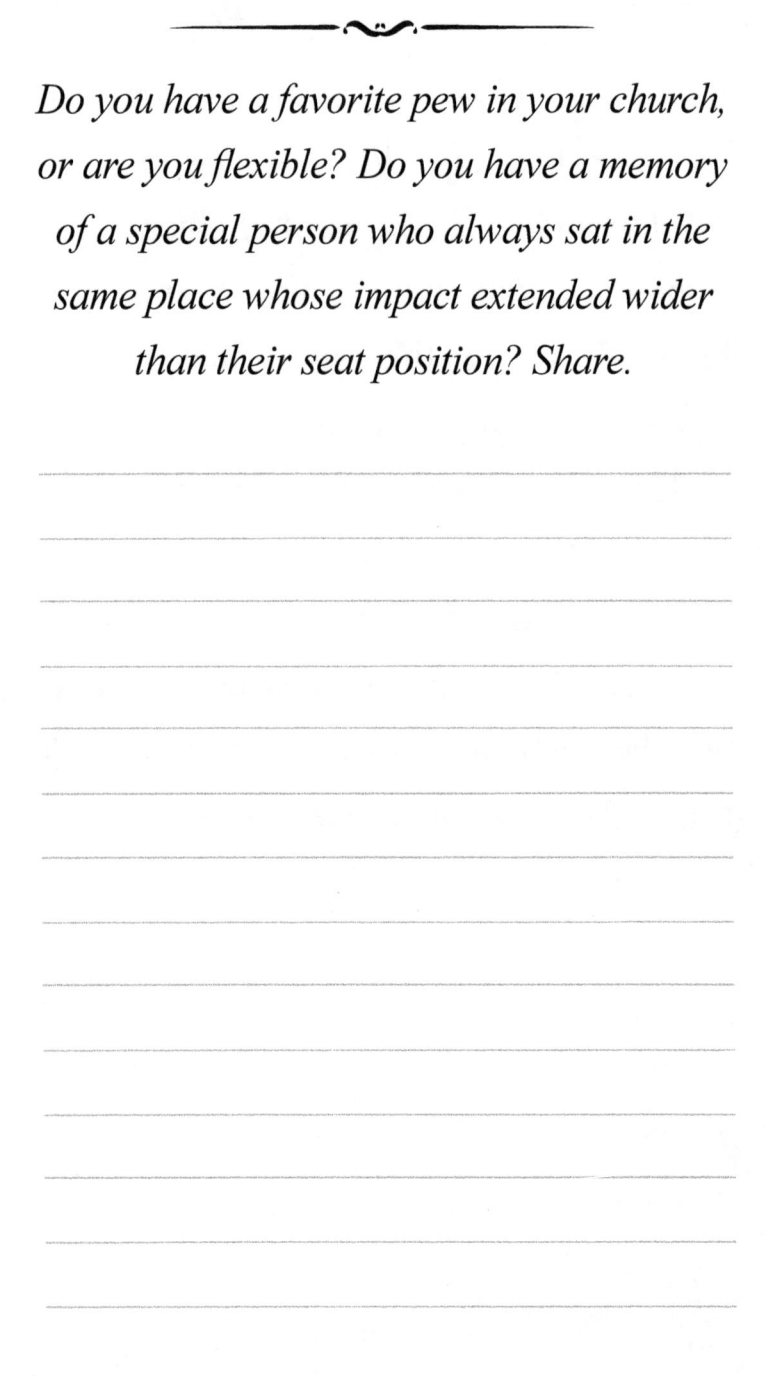

Do you have a favorite pew in your church, or are you flexible? Do you have a memory of a special person who always sat in the same place whose impact extended wider than their seat position? Share.

The Back Pew

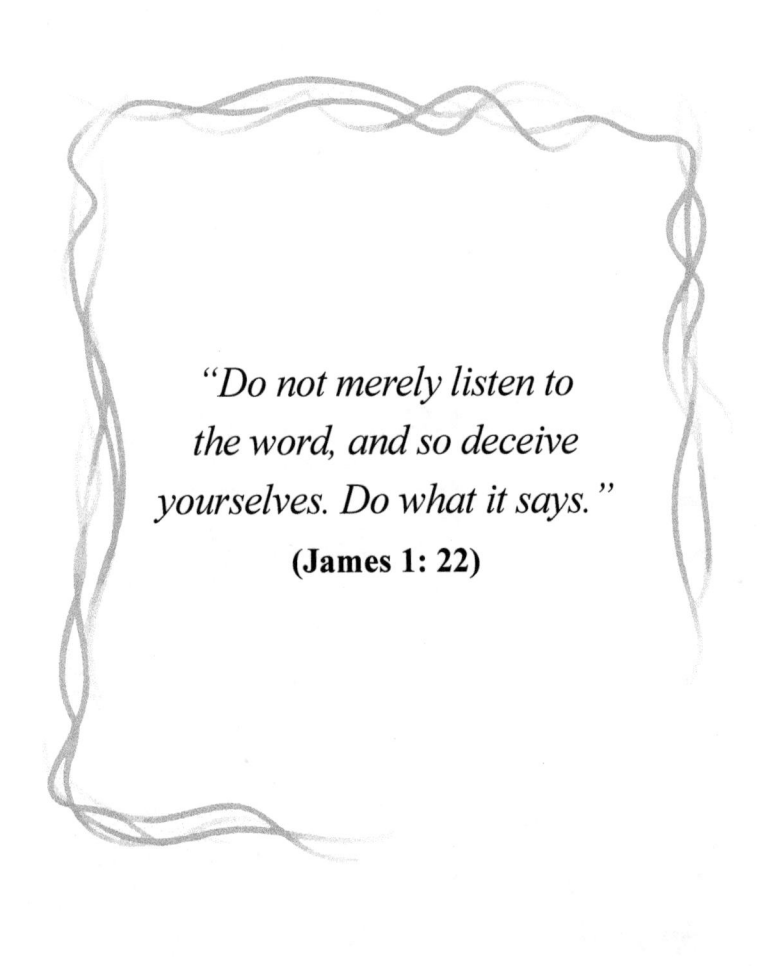

"Do not merely listen to the word, and so deceive yourselves. Do what it says."

(James 1: 22)

22

Know Your Faith

I was raised with both Baptist and Pentecostal faith influences. I was raised in the First Assembly of God, but we traveled a lot to other churches to sing. As I mentioned before, Daddy can sing and is gifted with an angel voice this side of heaven.

At a young age, he put me on stage with a microphone in my hand. Music was a special gift in my life, and it was wonderful to witness how the words of a song could move people to worship. I was blessed with two pastor uncles, and so the Word of God was in my life at every angle.

I was raised with a strong foundation of faith, but my faith was not a priority in my early adult years, between marriage and having kids. As I have gotten older, I am reminded that Jesus has never left me. He has always been with me, even when I wasn't giving him my life.

Thank goodness people never stopped praying for me. I am thankful I rededicated my life to Jesus and now make him a priority. I am grateful that I know him now more than ever. I look back and know he never forgot me.

I have attended many different churches, as our kids would connect with young groups and friends, but I have never forgotten my faith. No matter where you are today and what church you attend, know your faith. Know what you believe. Seek Jesus. "Seek and you shall find" is an often-used saying, but it's so true.

Seeking what he has for you starts with opening your heart. Pour into your heart by attending church, reading your Bible, doing Bible studies, and reading devotions. No matter where you are in your life and in your walk with Jesus, it's never too late to simply say yes to him. He wants to use you. Know your faith with confidence, and know your Jesus with boldness.

Open your heart to him and to his promises. No matter what comes your way, stand strong in his Word and know your faith. Share a bit about your faith.

Know Your Faith

*" 'I prayed for this child, and the L*ORD* has granted me what I asked of him. So now I give him to the L*ORD*. For his whole life he will be given over to the L*ORD*.' And he worshiped the L*ORD* there."*

(1 Samuel 1:27–28)

23

Baby Dedications

Baby dedications are some of my sweetest memories of my childhood at church. This was a simple, little service that usually happened on Sunday mornings at the end of service. Young parents would bring their new little one to the stage, and Uncle Laney would pray over the baby, the parents, and the family. He often gifted a Bible, with the date of dedication written in it.

Baby dedication wasn't only about the new little gift from God but also signified the parents and family dedicating themselves to raising the child in church under God and with thankfulness. As we had children, we dedicated each of them, committing to do our best to raise them right and teach them the way of the Lord.

Now as all my children are grown, I look at them and hold on to those precious moments of dedicating them to God. I am blessed with wonderful kids who have strong faith of their own. I look at them individually and know I did well instilling faith in them, and they use that in their own ways.

They will continue to explore their own faith as life carries on, but what we do as parents can influence them forever. I thank God every day my parents instilled faith in me when I was young. There was a time in my life when I put my faith in the back seat; but I returned to my Jesus, allowing him to take my wheel.

Being committed as a parent is the first step to good parenting. From birth to adulthood, you have an influence; and as a parent, it's up to you what you do with it. Children may not actually truly accept Jesus until later in life, but raise them to know he is always there.

Children are precious gifts from God and should be treated as such. It's solely on us parents to raise them in the ways of the Lord, their Creator. If you have raised your kids or are currently in survivor mode of raising them, know your Jesus cares for them. Cast your cares on him. He's waiting for you to do so.

Do you have a special memory of your children when they were little? Share.

Baby Dedications

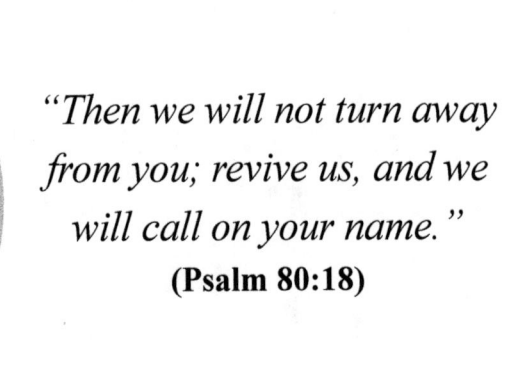

"Then we will not turn away from you; revive us, and we will call on your name."
(Psalm 80:18)

24

Revivals

Growing up Pentecostal in the Assembly of God church, revivals were just a regular part of our church goings. Special guest preachers would come to our church for several evenings in a row, and services would be held nightly.

The evangelist, as the preacher was called, seemed to preach a more powerful message than the church pastor; and you could guarantee when the altar call was given, people would respond. The Holy Spirit would move, there was powerful praise and worship, people would get prayed for, and sometimes there would be receiving the gift of the Holy Spirit.

Revivals always reminded me of what is described in the Bible on the day of Pentecost. Revivals were regular occurrences back when I was a girl. People from everywhere would visit the church where the revival was being held, even though it was a school night.

I saw people physically healed and hearts saved. It was always a beautiful moment when I got to witness someone ask Jesus Christ into their lives and make the decision to follow him. It was life-changing, and you could see the transformation happen in that person almost immediately.

Today revival is sweeping across the nation. I see TV news stories about revivals being held nightly for weeks. I see churches seeking more of their Jesus and praying for revival. I see people craving a closer walk with their Jesus and a movement in America that citizens want Jesus Christ to be back in our homes, schools, and businesses. I encourage you today to seek revival for yourself. Make Jesus a priority, and I promise he will show up. Revive us again and again, oh Lord!

Have you ever experienced a revival in your life? Have you been to a church service that moved your heart like never before, leaving you changed? Share.

Revivals

Final Thoughts

I am blessed to share a bit about the church of my childhood. I hope you have been blessed by reminiscing and that you have enjoyed sharing your own stories. No doubt the church has changed somewhat through my fifty-plus years of life, but I can assure you that my Jesus hasn't. I want to share some of my favorite thoughts. These thoughts have changed me in some way, and I am thankful.

"Trust in the Lord with all your heart and lean not on your own understanding" (Proverbs 3:5).

My best friend, Heather, battled breast cancer from the young age of thirty-four and lost her life at age thirty-eight. She held on to this verse in Proverbs as her lifeline during those four hard years.

We may not understand all that life brings our way, but we can learn to trust Jesus. Even if we try our hardest, life's trials still won't make sense, so simply learn to trust in his plan for your life, whatever it would be. I know it is easy for me to say because you may be going through something really tough, but I assure you, your Jesus is there.

"In the beginning God..." (Genesis 1:1). This revelation was brought to me by Pastor Mark Whitehead. Read those four powerful words. Read them again and again till they sink into your heart. God was at the start of creation, and if we apply

Final Thoughts

those same four words to everything we do in life, wonderful creations will come.

What a difference it would make if we included God in anything and everything. I am saying everything—not just the big religious things. Think on this and put it to action, and I promise you will see changes in your life journey.

My precious friend Elizabeth Mahusay, from McKinney, Texas, wrote a Bible study on the book of Philippians, *Transform My Thinking, God: Six Principles to Beat Negative Thinking and Build a Life You Want.* This study changed my life and the way I thought on things.

Philippians is the story of Paul, who we know ended up in jail. Paul shared the word of God and preached the gospel, and where did it get him? In a jail cell. Paul could have sat there and cursed God for allowing him to be imprisoned, but he didn't. Paul made the most of his situation and ministered from his jail cell to those who would listen—the other prisoners and guards. And Paul kept on preaching.

So many times, life just doesn't go according to our plans; and we sit on our duffs and puff. We get angry that our God allowed this to happen, and some even turn away from their Jesus. But from this study, I learned to open my eyes to see what my Jesus wants me to see. I learned not question him with, "Why, Lord?" I learned to simply open my heart to the opportunities being given to me and then to do something with those opportunities.

Life won't always go perfectly, but God never leaves us. These are the times he wants us to trust him even more and know he is there. In every single situation, every

Final Thoughts

place you go or every journey he takes you on, he is there. I had to learn to say yes.

When you follow Jesus, he may take you to some uncomfortable places; but learn to open your heart and say yes. And trust in your Father. You may not have considered going or doing those things if he had not shaken up your life otherwise.

So think of Paul's story and learn to say yes. Remember, life was never promised to be perfect, but he created you for his purpose. Yes, you. Read that again and let it sink in. You were created for his purpose.

I pray blessings for each of you as you hold your memories and thoughts close. I pray that what you have shared touches the lives of your loved ones for generations to come. Your life is worth documenting, so thank you for sharing with others.

If you ever find yourself in East Texas, look me up! Gladewater is officially titled the "Antique Capital of East Texas." You can find me most days downtown at my store, The Byrd's Nest. Come sit a spell and let's visit. I will be more than happy to share my testimony and my memories with you.

Until then, be blessed.

Hugs,
Mrs. Karla

Order Information

REDEMPTION PRESS

Additional copies of this book can be ordered wherever Christian books are sold.